Lives and Times

Ben Cohen

The Founder of Ben & Jerry's Ice Cream

M.C. Hall

Heinemann Library
Chicago, Illinois

Customer Service 888-454-2279
Visit our website at www.heinemannlibrary.com

Designed by Richard Parker and Maverick Design
Photo research by Julie Laffin
Printed and bound in China by South China Printing Company Limited

09 08 07 06 05
10 9 8 7 6 5 4 3 2 1

Library of Congress Cataloging-in-Publication Data
Hall, Margaret, 1947-
    Ben Cohen and the beginning of Ben & Jerry's ice cream / M.C. Hall.
        p. cm. -- (Lives and times)
    Includes bibliographical references and index.
    ISBN 1-4034-6349-2 (lib. bdg.) -- ISBN 1-4034-6363-8 (pbk.)
1. Cohen, Ben (Ben R.)--Juvenile literature. 2. Greenfield,
Jerry--Juvenile literature. 3. Ben & Jerry's (Firm)--History--Juvenile
literature. 4. Businesspeople--United States--Biography--Juvenile
literature. 5. Ice cream industry--United States--History--Juvenile
literature. I. Title. II. Series: Lives and times (Des Plaines, Ill.)
    HD9281.U52C644 2005
    338.7'6374'092--dc22

                        2004021935

Acknowledgments
The author and publishers are grateful to the following for permission to reproduce copyright material:
p. 4 David Young-Wolff/Photo Edit; pp. 5, 23, 26 Getty Images; p. 6 Erich Hartmann/Magnum Photos; p. 7 Janet Lankford Moran/Heinemann Library; p. 8 Time Life Pictures/Getty Images; p. 9 Underwood & Underwood/Corbis; pp. 10, 11, 12 Corbis; p. 13 J. Graham/Robertstock.com; p. 14 Hulton Archive/Getty Images; p. 15, 18, 19 AP Wide World Photos; p. 16 James P. Blair/Corbis; p. 17 © Robert Grego. All rights reserved Vermont Photo Creations; p. 20 © Richard Levine; p. 21 Joe Sohm/The Image Works; p. 22 Andrew E. Cook; pp. 24, 27 Photri Microstock; p. 25 Robert Holmes/Corbis

Cover photograph by Getty Images

Cover and interior icons Janet Lankford Moran/Heinemann Library

Some words are shown in bold, **like this**. You can find out what they mean by looking in the glossary.

Contents

We All Like Ice Cream! 4

The Early Years 6

Ben Meets Jerry 8

College Years 10

A Teaching Job 12

Looking for Ideas 14

Getting Started 16

The First Ice Cream Parlor 18

Ben & Jerry's Grows 20

Helping Others 22

The Later Years 24

Ben Today 26

Fact File 28

Timeline 29

Glossary 30

More Books to Read 31

Index 32

We All Like Ice Cream!

People around the world love ice cream. This cold treat comes in many different flavors. People eat ice cream in cones, bars, and as a dessert.

Ice cream is one of the world's favorite foods!

When he was a boy, Ben Cohen loved ice cream. When he grew up, he started an ice cream **company** with his best friend, Jerry Greenfield. They made and sold **unusual** flavors of ice cream.

This is Ben on the right, with his best friend Jerry.

The Early Years

Ben Cohen was born in Brooklyn, New York, in 1951. His father was an **accountant**. His mother took care of Ben and his sister, Alice. When Ben was young, the family moved to Merrick, New York.

This is how Brooklyn looked in the 1950s.

Ben and his father both loved ice cream. Ben's father could finish an entire half gallon after dinner!

Ben liked to add things, like pieces of cookies and candy, to his ice cream.

Ben Meets Jerry

When Ben was in seventh grade, he became best friends with Jerry Greenfield. During the summers, they earned money by sorting mail at the office of Ben's father.

Ben and Jerry liked to go to the nearby beach with their friends.

In his last year of high school, Ben got a job driving an ice cream truck, selling ice cream. In 1969, Ben started college at Colgate University in Hamilton, New York.

Ben sold his ice cream from a truck like this one.

College Years

Ben didn't like college, so he quit and traveled to California. He worked there as an "ice cream man." After a few months, he went back to New York.

Ben got a job driving cabs just like these all over New York.

Ben enjoyed making clay pots.

Ben took **pottery** and jewelry classes at Skidmore College in Saratoga Springs, New York. In 1972, he moved to New York City to work as a potter.

A Teaching Job

In 1974, Ben started to teach at a school for troubled teenagers. He taught them **pottery**, photography, film making, and other **crafts**.

The school was close to the Adirondack mountains in New York State.

On the right is an ice cream maker. Ben used one like this to make ice cream for the students.

Ben also worked as the school cook. Sometimes he made ice cream for the students. In 1976, the school closed. Ben was out of a job again!

Looking for Ideas

Ben and his old friend, Jerry Greenfield, decided to start a **company** together. Ben and Jerry both liked to eat. They wanted to have a food company.

Ben and Jerry knew that other people liked to eat too!

Here are Jerry and Ben
scooping ice cream.

At first, Ben and Jerry thought about
opening a restaurant. Then they decided
they wanted to make and sell ice cream
instead.

Getting Started

Ben and Jerry looked for a place to start their **company**. They chose Burlington, Vermont. There were no **ice cream parlors** in Burlington. Theirs would be the first.

There is a big university in Burlington. Ben and Jerry knew college students liked ice cream!

Ben and Jerry borrowed some money to buy an old gas station. They spent months fixing it up. They also took classes to learn more about making ice cream.

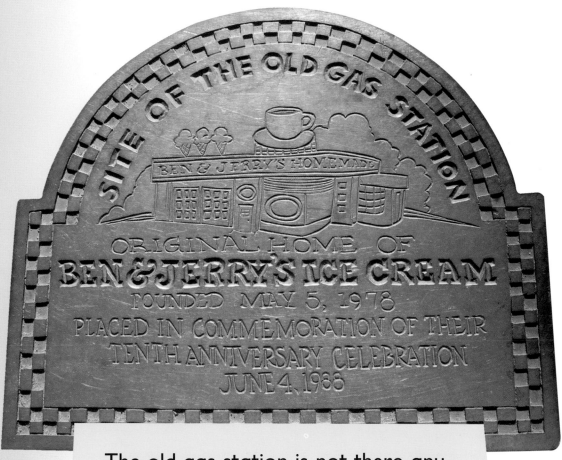

SITE OF THE OLD GAS STATION

BEN & JERRY'S HOMEMADE

ORIGINAL HOME OF
BEN & JERRY'S ICE CREAM
FOUNDED MAY 5, 1978
PLACED IN COMMEMORATION OF THEIR
TENTH ANNIVERSARY CELEBRATION
JUNE 4, 1988

The old gas station is not there any more. Today there is only this plaque in the sidewalk to show where it was.

The First Ice Cream Parlor

Ben & Jerry's Homemade **Ice Cream Parlor** opened on May 5, 1978. The store served **unusual** flavors, such as Coconut and Honey Almond Mist. People tried their ice cream, and loved it.

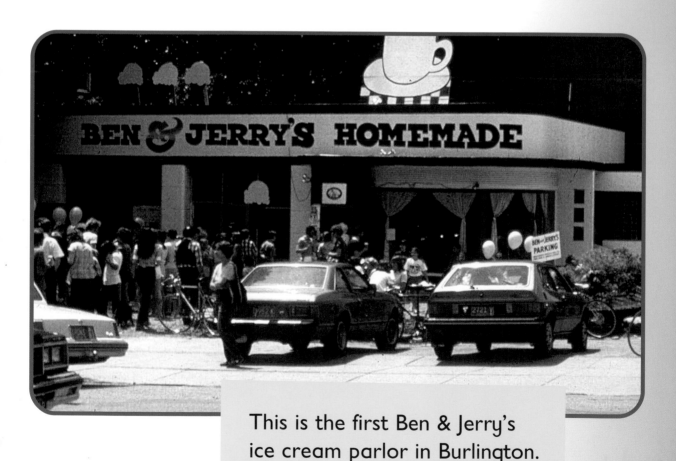

This is the first Ben & Jerry's ice cream parlor in Burlington.

At first Ben and Jerry did most jobs themselves. When the **company** grew, they moved into a bigger space.

Soon Ben and Jerry started selling their ice cream to grocery stores.

19

Ben & Jerry's Grows

Other people wanted to start their own Ben & Jerry's **ice cream parlors**. The owners of the new ice cream parlors paid Ben and Jerry money to use their names.

The first store run by someone other than Ben and Jerry opened in Shelbourne, Vermont in 1981.

This is the Ben & Jerry's factory in Waterbury, Vermont.

In 1986, Ben and Jerry opened a **factory** near Waterbury, Vermont. They sold so much ice cream, they soon opened another factory in Springfield, Vermont.

Helping Others

Ben and Jerry decided that their **business** would give away part of the money it made every year. The money would go to help people and groups in the **community**.

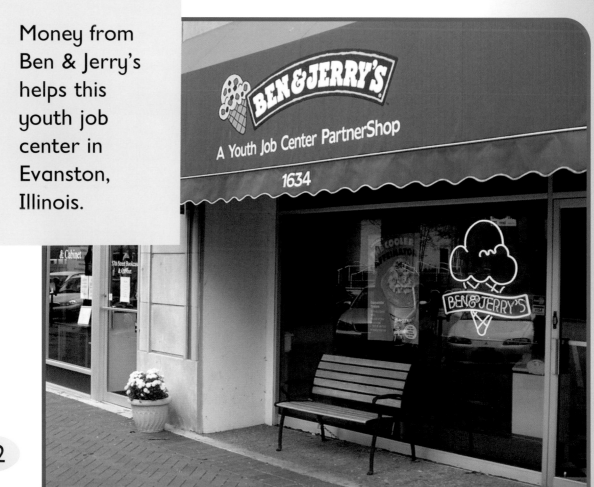

Money from Ben & Jerry's helps this youth job center in Evanston, Illinois.

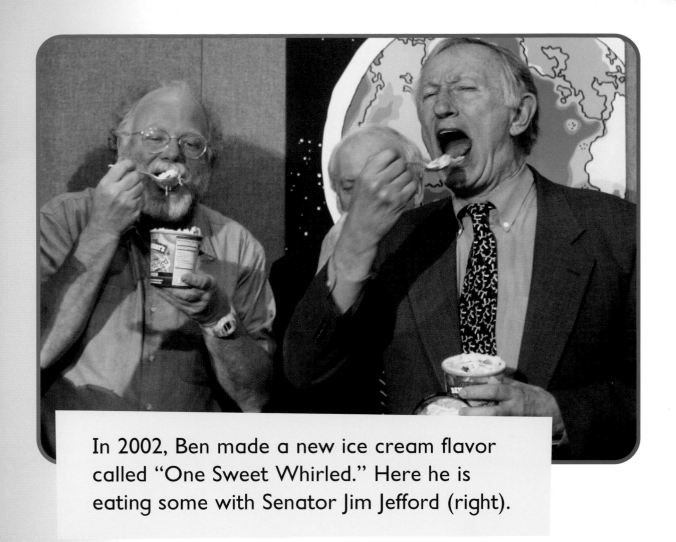

In 2002, Ben made a new ice cream flavor called "One Sweet Whirled." Here he is eating some with Senator Jim Jefford (right).

Ben also believes that companies should work to save the **environment**. He had the idea to use rain forest nuts in his ice cream. Then people would not cut down the nut trees. In 2002 Ben joined the fight against **global warming**.

The Later Years

Ben and Jerry wanted their workers to be happy and have fun. They won awards for the way they ran their **company**, and for helping the **environment**.

Every year, Ben and Jerry liked to meet with the people who supported their company.

In 2000 Ben and Jerry sold their company to a large food maker. Ben does not work for Ben & Jerry's Ice Cream now. He still does **community** work to help people.

Ben and Jerry's famous Cowmobile still travels around to many community projects.

Ben Today

Today Ben works hard for a group that he started, called True Majority. True Majority tries to get **laws** passed by the U.S. **government** that will help children, the **environment**, and the world.

Ben makes speeches to get people to **vote** on paper— not on computers. He wants to make sure that every person's vote is counted.

THE COMPUTER ATE MY VOTE

Ben's ice cream is famous around the world. You can learn more about his **company** by visiting the **factory** near Waterbury, Vermont.

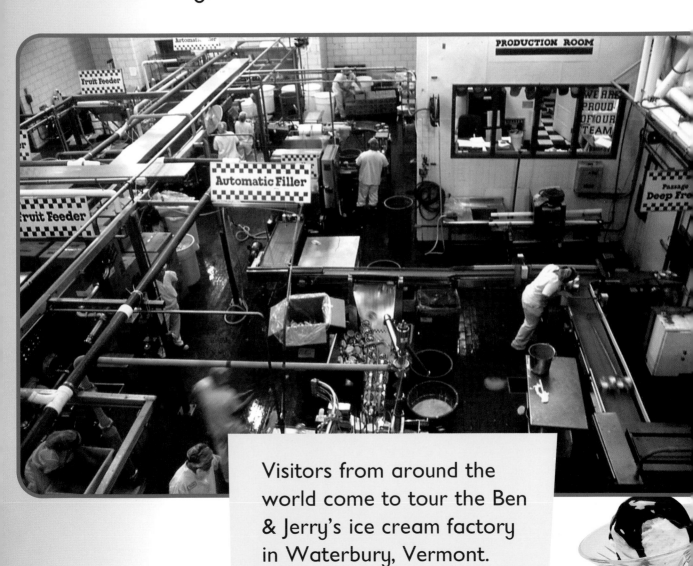

Visitors from around the world come to tour the Ben & Jerry's ice cream factory in Waterbury, Vermont.

27

Fact File

- Ben and Jerry paid $5 to take a class and learn how to make ice cream. They took the class by mail.

- In 1999 Ben & Jerry's celebrated 21 years of ice-cream making by giving away ice cream across the United States. Their **company** gave away more than half a million cones!

- Ben Cohen was married for a time. He and his former wife, Cindy, have one daughter, named Aretha.

- One of Ben's hobbies is riding motorcycles. He likes to ride around the Vermont countryside.

Timeline

1951   Ben Cohen is born in Brooklyn, New York

1963   Ben meets Jerry Greenfield

1972   Ben moves to New York City

1978   Ben and Jerry open their first **Ice Cream Parlor** in Burlington, Vermont

1980   Ben and Jerry start selling ice cream to grocery stores

1981   Ben and Jerry start to let other people pay to open their own Ben & Jerry's Ice Cream Parlors

1985   Ben and Jerry build an ice cream **factory** near Waterbury, Vermont
Ben and Jerry start the Ben & Jerry's Foundation to give away money for **community** projects

1994   Ben & Jerry's begins selling ice cream in Great Britain

1995   Ben and Jerry open a new factory in St. Albans, Vermont

2000   Ben and Jerry sell the **company**

Glossary

accountant person who keeps track of money for a business

business trade or activity that earns money

company group of people who make money by selling something

community town or city where people live or work

crafts activities that are done with the hands, such as sewing or pottery

environment the world around you. Water, plants, and air are all part of the environment.

factory building in which things are made

government group that leads a country and makes laws

global warming the idea that Earth's temperature is rising, making weather change all over the world

ice cream parlor place where people can buy and eat ice cream

law the rules of a country

pottery making things, like dishes and pots, from clay

unusual strange

vote give support to something or someone

More Books to Read

An older reader can help you with these books:

Pickering, Robin. *I Like Ice Cream*. San Francisco, CA: Children's Press, 2000.

Snyder, Inez. *Milk to Ice Cream*. San Francisco, CA: Children's Press, 2003.

Fleisher, Paul. *Ice Cream Treats: The Inside Scoop*. Minneapolis, MN: Carolrhoda Books, 2001.

Keller, Kristin. *Milk to Ice Cream*. Mankata, MN: Capstone Press, 2005.

Landau, Elaine. *Ice Cream: The Cold Creamy Treat*. Vero Beach, FL: Rourke, 2001.

Older, Jules. *Ice Cream: Including Great Moments in Ice Cream History*. Watertown, MA: Charlesbridge Publishing, 2002.

Index

birth 6, 29

Cohen, Aretha 28

Cohen, Cindy 28

college 9, 10

community 22, 25

company 14, 16, 19, 23, 24, 25, 27, 28, 29

environment 23, 24, 26

factory 21, 27

family 6

Greenfield, Jerry 5, 8, 14, 15, 16, 28, 29

ice cream 4, 5, 7, 9, 10, 13, 15, 16, 17, 18, 19, 28, 29

pottery 11, 12

teaching 12